Alan Murphy was born in Dublin on the last day of the sixties. [He lives in the in]sane town of Lismore, County Waterford, where he accumulates poems an[d pictures. He has] a diploma in Fine Art, and has exhibited his artwork in numerous locatio[ns. Before entering the] alternative universe of children's poetry he published a number of "seriou[s" poems for adults and] wrote some comedy monologues and sketches. He has given many public readings of his poems.

Publications/Reviews

Psychosilly is his second book. His first book **The Mona Lisa's on our Fridge** was reviewed in the **Irish Times** as one of the best children's poetry books of 2009.

PRAISE FOR **THE MONA LISA'S ON OUR FRIDGE**

"Quirky, funny and eccentric…cheerful and colourful…well crafted and thought out. [The poems] use a vocabulary which does not patronise the reader and will probably expand his or hers." **Books Ireland**

"The Picasso of Irish poetry…you never cease to be amazed by the explosion of colourful words and vivid imagery created by the poet." **The Avondhu**

"It deserves to do well. I like where [he's] coming from!…The illustrations are great." **Arthur Mathews** co-author of Father Ted

"I love books like [this] that defy categorisation…there is a crazy wackiness about this publication that I really like…relax the mind and enjoy!" **Theresa Doran** Books Ireland

"Nine out of ten." **Colm Power** aged 11

www.avantcardpublications.com

First published in Ireland by **AvantCard Publications**, 2011
All rights reserved ©Text and images copyright 2011 Alan Murphy

A CIP catalogue record for this book is available from the British Library ISBN 978 0 9561734 1 6
Layout by Ronan Hayes, design by Alan Murphy. Printed by City Print Tel: 021 454 5655
AvantCard Publications, 41 The Mills, Lismore, Co. Waterford, Ireland. Tel: +353 (0)87 683 5873

Alan Murphy

PsychoSilly

AvantCard Publications

Acknowledgments

A big thank you to **Susan Knight**, **Jay Roche**, **Muireann**, **Seamus Cashman** and **Robert Dunbar**, to **Tricia Lewis, Deirdre Lewis**, **Carol Ann Duffy**, **Liam Murphy**, **Christy Parker**, **Antonia Zane**, **Da**, **Inka Design**, **The Mad Art Gallery**, the **Tyrone Guthrie Centre**, the **Irish M.E. Trust**, **Brid MacSweeney** and **Jenni Duggan**, to **Jane**, **Catherine**, **Maureen Ryan**, **Sha Griffin**, the Libraries of Dublin, Cork, Waterford and Lismore, all **FB friends** and everyone else who has voiced encouragement along the way. Most of all I am indebted to **Ronan** for his support and assistance in putting this book together.

The **Henri Bergson** quotation (from "L'Evolution Creatice",1907) was spotted in **The Penguin International Thesaurus of Quotations**, compiled by Rhoda Thomas Tripp, 1970.

Apologies to two members of the **Davis family** for the use of their names, and to **Ryan Tubridy** for the use of his nose.

"Intelligence is characterized by a natural incomprehension of life." Henri Bergson

Contents

The Doodle Man	10
Ogre! Ogre!	12
If My Body Is A Temple	14
An Alien From Inner Space	16
Nature's All Naked	18
Snuffed Out	21
Psychosilly	23
The Chalk And Cheese Of The Universe	24
Why Do I Dream?	26
As A Matter Of Fantasy	28
A Numbskull	31
Where Do The Dead Go When They Die?	33
Step Out Of Your Skin	34
The History Of The Sandwich	37
Ham Sandwich Haiku	38
In Praise Of Buttocks	39
A Limerick In…	40
The Pig And The Parasol	42
Down Our Alleyway	44
Which Came First?	47
Senseless	48
Right As Rain	49
Ode To Blue Tack	50
Piece Of Mind	51
Rhyme Is The Reason	52
Green Vegetables	54
Hell Is Homework	56
Funny Phrases	58
Our Dog Is Dreaming	61
Your Common Or Garden Martian	62
Buttons And Puddles And Mud And Chairs	64
The Pineapple Republic	67

THE DOODLE MAN

The Doodle Man is what I am;
I'm brought to life in lazy classrooms,
I dwell in the margins and squat on corners,
I'm drawn for fun on any blank space:

A zig-zag line, well that's my mouth;
On top of that a spiral nose,
Two asterisk eyes, a half-pint head,
A sketchy body, thumbnail clothes.

Small is beautiful, that's my creed;
I shout it but you do not heed;
I'm dwarfed by your dreaming pen
That conjures capers once again.

The Doodle Man is what I am;
Made up of wonky geometry;
A face that peers from shapes and swirls,
Pen product of a scribble world.

The Doodle guy with a suit and tie,
A Doodle wife, a Doodle home,
In a Doodle city one inch wide,
A humble hamlet on the side.

But if all doodles in the world
Were gathered on one single sheet
That screed might stretch to Timbuktu;
Now wouldn't that be something new?

A Doodle country, by decree,
Surrounded by a Doodle sea,
On a Doodle planet crammed with cartoons
Spinning round with Doodle glee!

The Doodle Man is what I am;
I'm one long daydream from cloud nine,
I'll break the ice on your new schoolbooks;
Japes and skits and tricks I'll mime.

The Doodle Man is what I am;
That's right; stick figure to the stars,
All improvised and global too
And coming soon to a page near you.

OGRE! OGRE!

Ogre! Ogre! Coming this way!
It wobbles and lurches and bobs and sways,
It's fat as a fiddle that's far too big,
With sharp teeth and nails and large horns you won't dig.
Not nice.

It's probably never been to a gym.
It probably wouldn't sing you a hymn.
It's out on its own and it's out on a limb,
Forging a furious fate!

Ogre! Ogre! Coming our way!
Run for the hills, get out of the way!
See the earth under it tremble and shake,
Forcing a virtual Ogre-quake!
Watch out!

He probably wouldn't sing you a song.
He probably isn't friendly for long.
He'd eat you for breakfast and think nothing wrong.
Some chum!

Ogres, Ogres, nasty it's true,
Coming soon to a town near you;
Don't cover yourself in pepper but pray
That this one's had dinner already today.
Some hope!

They'll eat twelve kids inside of an hour.
And never once stop to pick a nice flower.
Their habits are mean and their temper is dour.
That's monsters for you!

And this one's never been for a bath.
He'd bite of your head just as soon as he'd laugh,
So disappear quickly unless you are daft!
It's Ogres' day today!

IF MY BODY IS A TEMPLE…

If my body is a temple
Then my nose is a church,
With my ears as two car parks
To leave traffic in the lurch.

If my body is a temple
Then my stomach is a sieve,
And my feet can be frying pans
With sausages that live.

If my body is a temple
Then my mind is a maze
For kids to wander and to ponder
On summer days.

If my body is a temple
Then my bottom is a bus
To take me all around the town
When I'm in a rush.

If my body is a temple
Then my tongue is a track
For food to follow what I swallow
Like coins dropped in a sack.

If my body is a temple
Then my knees are like notes
Of music in a silver song,
With lyrics you can quote.

If my body is a temple
Then my hair is like hail;
It comes down when the sky's a scissors
Again and again.

If my body is a temple
Then my bones are a beard;
They wrap their white around the night
When things get weird.

If my body is a temple
Then where the hell's the door?
And what on earth are arms and legs
And heads and torsos for?!!

AN ALIEN FROM INNER SPACE

An Alien from Inner Space,

Between the ears, behind the face,

A dreamling dreamt up in a trance;

A traveller come to earth by chance.

He won't add up or go to school,
He's happy to break all the rules;
He floats and fools and speaks in tongues
As that's his way of having fun.

He's the antenna of an ant,
The cool complexion of a plant,
His eyes are pickled jellyfish,
He's here to grant our every wish.

I like to spend my days when free
Laughing at his levity,
And watch him juggle asteroids
Or spy him sailing through the void.

I see him now in Inner Space,
Can visualise his oddball face,
Anatomy and far-out clothes;
Just where he gets them no one knows.

He'll always be a friend in need;
I'll always heed his cosmic creed,
Till he floats off one final time…

And all I'm left with is this rhyme.

NATURE'S ALL NAKED

Nature's all naked,
The shrubs and the trees,
The mountains and valleys,
The birds and the bees.

Humans wear knickers,
Some socks and a scarf
And a big woolly jumper
When evenings get dark.

Badgers are bashful
But never put on
A stitch of crude clothing,
At least not for long.

Snails are cerebral
And stay in their shells
When bug-bodies creep round
With garments to sell.

Have you ever see the ocean squeeze
Into a pair of jeans to please
The fashionable frivolities
Of men and women too?

Yet if you try to ape the beasts:
The cats , the dogs, the ducks, the geese,
You may feel left out in the cold
Or end up in a zoo!

Lizards are lazy
In midday sun's glare,
Scorning sun lotion
Cause it they don't wear.

Donkeys though drastic
When worked to the bone
Still settle for saddles
And leave suits alone.

Have you ever seen a mountain try
To put sunglasses on its eye,
Even if the sun came out
and said it looks real cool?

Yet if you settle in the grass,
No fabric facing your bare ass,
And something bites you where it hurts,
It's you who'll look the fool!

Wombats are wicked
To earwigs and ants,
But never crash parties
In flash leather pants.

Dolphins though dashing
And frisky as well,
Are not fashion conscious
And it suits them well.

Nature's all naked,
The shrubs and the trees,
The mountains and valleys,
The birds and the bees.

Nature's all naked,
All green and all blue,
As clear as the daylight's
Summery hue.

SNUFFED OUT

Bitten by an apple,
Beaten up by an egg,
Sat on by a sumptuous chair,
And combed in fact by a lock of hair.

Put out by the cat,
Walked on by the grass,
Chewed up by some chewing gum,
But figured out by a difficult sum.

Stolen by some gold,
Kicked about by a ball,
Discarded by some tattered clothes,
Yet sniffed at by a fragrant rose.

Mixed up by some cement,
Cooked by a bowl of soup,
Finished by a game,
And snuffed out by a flame.

PSYCHOSILLY

Psychosilly;
A boy without a brain,
A fish without a skeleton,
A sink without a drain.

Psychosilly;
A girl without a bean,
A land that's mellow, yellow, jello,
A sky that's gone all green.

A laugh without a mouth,
A dream without a doubt,
A wobbling hobbling universe,
But what's it all about?

Psychosilly;
A man without a mind;
A poet without principles,
Except the loopy kind.

THE CHALK AND CHEESE OF THE UNIVERSE

The Chalk of the Universe

      writes its rhymes on the blackboard of space.

      is a rock on the dark side of the moon.

      is the colour of clowns all over the galaxy.

      is not in the recipe books.

The Cheese of the Universe
        Is dissected by hungry scientists.
        smells like alien's brain.
        sizzles when it gets too close to the sun.
        is short on conversation but long in the mouth.

One day when the world was young as a wish,
Some cheese was put in a satellite dish;
Some chalk was added as a surprise…

There was a Big Bang -

And that's the way the universe lies.

WHY DO I DREAM?

Why did I dream that a garden was growing inside my head?

Why did I dream that peas were purple and milk was red?

Why did I dream that the day began when I went off to bed?

Why did I dream that antelopes were sipping on drinks?
Why did I dream that artichokes were slipping me winks?
Bedtime is strange and quite screwy, methinks.

Why did I dream that the cat went to college and earned a degree?
Why did I dream that the universe was the size of a flea?
Why did I dream that the sea was saved in a large cup of tea?

And why did I dream that the clouds were real in a baby's room?
Why did I dream that the sky was snowy in the month of June?
Why did I dream of a fish that went by in a hot air balloon?

How did I dream that I put all my clothes on in two seconds flat?
How did I dream that my schoolbag changed itself into a bat?
How did I dream that I ate lots of chocolate without getting fat?

When did I dream that the world would end and that school would be out?
When did I dream that children would take over towns with a shout?
When did I dream that the moon would be candy in everyone's mouth?

Why do I dream but none of my wishes ever come true?
Why do I dream and then wake up and find that the world is anew?
Why do I lose last nights lunacy soon as it's through?

Why, why, why do I dream?

AS A MATTER OF FANTASY…

As a matter of fantasy
The sun is square, it's plain to see,
Clouds are yellow and grass is blue
And the wind blows kisses for me and you.

As a matter of fantasy
The garden's growing upside down,
With flowers buried deep in their beds
While their dark roots tower above our heads.

As a matter of fantasy
The dinner's made of steam today;
Water's concrete and chips are bricks
And a dog-faced cat is licking its lips.

As a matter of fantasy
The stars are stabbing the street tonight;
They've finally fallen down to earth,
They're glowing and glistening in the dirt.

As a matter of fantasy
I hailed a taxi made of twine;
I sat inside as it roamed and unravelled
And disappeared by the end of my travels.

As a matter of fantasy
Our local church was furnished with wheels;
Praying is possible only for those
Who follow the building wherever it goes.

As a matter of fantasy
The sun is square, it's plain to see,
Clouds are yellow and grass is blue
And the wind blows wonders for me and you.

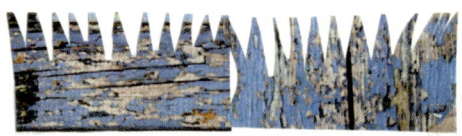

A NUMBSKULL

A numbskull climbed a hill of beans
And watched a paper aeroplane
Take off into a vermilion sky
Whose vivid hue was just a dye.

He slid back down to a tinfoil earth,
A place devoid of grass or dirt,
And if you think he's flesh and blood
Then think again, he's made of mud!

WHERE DO THE DEAD GO WHEN THEY DIE?

Where do the dead go when they die?
Is it to heaven or hell that they fly?
Is a rough grave their final bed?
Do they live on inside our heads?

Where do the dead go when they die?
What realm receives their final sigh?
Is it a void or is it pure light?
A tenacious boon come to put things right?

What do the living see in a ghost?
A spectre, a spook, an imp or a hoax?
What level of laughter is heard from beyond?
What type of terror makes humans go wan?

If a firm answer lies beyond our grasp
We'll just have to wait until that final gasp,
But don't count the days (it might make life a chore);
There's plenty of things here on earth to live for!

STEP OUT OF YOUR SKIN

Step out of your skin
Become a butterfly

Step out of your skin
Inhabit a hare

Step out of your skin
Take over a tiger

Step out of your skin
Swap souls with a bear

Step out of your skin
Enlarge to an elephant

Step out of your skin
Shrink down to a snail

Step out of your skin
Change into a cheetah

Step out of your skin
Transform to a whale

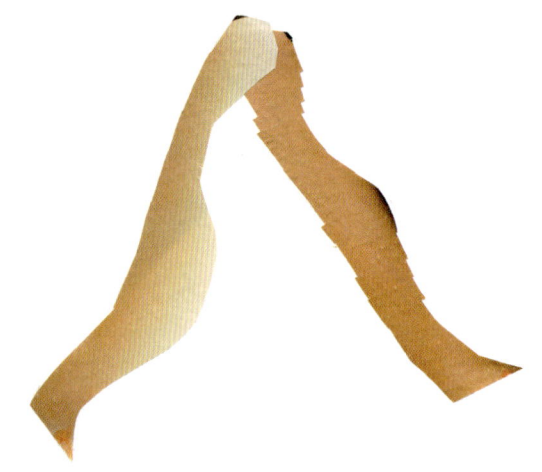

Step out of your skin
And mimic a mammoth

Step out of your skin
And imitate ants

Step out of your skin
Impersonate pumas

Step out of your skin
And give it a chance

Step out of your skin
Disguise as a dolphin

Step out of your skin
Dress up as a deer

Step out of your skin
Costume as a cobra

Step out of your skin
There's nothing to fear

Step out of your skin
Become a great ocean

Step out of your skin
Become a great tree

Step out of your skin
Enchant the whole universe

Step out of your skin
And do it with me.

THE HISTORY OF THE SANDWICH

By the ancient Nile
Cleopatra dined
By tucking in
To a crocodile bun?

In the holy land
A rabbi planned
A Passover snack
And a lunch was packed.

Lord Sandwich knew
That his name was right
When he finally took
That fateful bite.

And now everyday
The Wisdom of the Ages
Resides between
Two fresh-cut pages.

HAM SANDWICH HAIKU

The meat lies between
Bread that I've chosen to wed;
Rest in peace porcus.

IN PRAISE OF BUTTOCKS

Normally they come in twos;
They stand at bus stops or sit on loos,
They sometimes wobble when you walk,
And though they part they do not talk.

Buttocks are fine, buttocks are good,
Buttocks are part of the neighbourhood,
Every man should have a pair,
A standard lamp and a comfy chair.

Some praise ears or chins or knees,
Overlooking their bottoms expertise,
The time is past to turn the other cheek,
It's love and respect that buttocks seek!

Firm or wobbly, fat or thin,
Those swellings will always make me grin,
Like hillocks of pleasure that happily chime,
They're humble yet noble, they're yours and they're mine.

No matter what happens or fate that befalls
In towns and in cities, in houses and halls,
They'll always be there like two faithful friends,
Pert partners in crime until the end.

A LIMERICK IN…

1. Lismore

There was a old man from Lismore
Who walked right into a door,
This much we can tell;
His nose it did swell,
And that he let out a great roar.

2. Waterford

A headstrong young lady from Waterford
Thought that to marry was quite absurd,
She'd ride to the gates
But make sure the fates
Didn't one fraction further let her be lured.

3. Cork

Did you hear of the traveller from Cork
Who journeyed to China by fork?
It catapulted him
To Tiananmen
Where he landed with a loud report.

4. Kerry

I once knew a farmer from Kerry
Who's face was as round as a berry,
Bright red it was too
For cows with a view
To see in the dark where to hurry.

5. Limerick

If you set a limerick in Limerick
Your wits they have to be quick.
To distinguish of course
Between town and verse;
A marriage, like fiddle and fiddlestick.

THE PIG AND THE PARASOL

The Pig and the Parasol,
The umbrella and the eel,
A rhino in a ra-ra skirt
And a cigar for a seal.

An aardvark in an elevator,
A badger on a bus,
A field mouse on a ferry boat
That ought to be for us.

A banana in a bikini,
A pair of trousers for a tree,
A worm with its own wardrobe
Could be just like you or me.

DOWN OUR ALLEYWAY

Have you ever seen a vampire playing golf?
Or a ghoul from a sarcophagus called Rolf?
Have you ever drank a cup of cyanide
With a tasty chocolate biscuit on the side?

I have ,yes, I've seen it all down our alleyway;
Seen it, spied it, glimpsed it once or twice.
I have, yes, I've seen it all on a rainy day;
Strange scenes made to baffle and entice.

Have you ever seen a banshee with a bloke?
Or a mummy take a suntan on a slope?
Have you ever dropped in on a drowsy bat,
Curled up calmly by the fire like a cat?

I have, yes, I've seen it all down our alleyway;
Seen it, spied it, glimpsed it once or twice.
I have, yes, I've seen it all on a rainy day;
Strange scenes made to baffle and entice.

Have you ever travelled to the depths of hell,
And taken lots of photographs as well?
Have you ever witnessed medieval torture
On a game show with applause and happy laughter?

I have, yes, I've seen it all down our alleyway;
Seen it, spied it, glimpsed it once or twice.
I have, yes, I've seen it all on a rainy day;
Strange scenes made to baffle and entice.

And how about the castle of a count
In the summer when the sun has just popped out?
Or the vision of a monster on the move
At a disco to a funky fiendish groove?

Yes, it's true, I've seen it all down our alleyway;
Seen it, spied it, glimpsed it once or twice.
And if you see the same things too on a rainy day,
Ignore all the above, that's my advice!

WHICH CAME FIRST?

Which came first? The chicken or the egg?
Which came first? The body or the head?
Which came first? The living or the dead?

Which came first? The ice cream or the cone?
Which came first? The doggy or the bone?
Which came first? The telly or the phone?

Which came first? The door key or its lock?
Which came first? The shepherd or his flock?
Which came first? A hard place or a rock?

Which came first? The blue sky or the cloud?
Which came first? The cadaver or the shroud?
Which came first? The valley or the mound?

Which came first? The beginning or the end?
Which came first? Bitter foe or bosom friend?
Which came first? The roadway or its bend?

Which came first? The landmass or the sea?
Which came first? Was it bird or was it bee?
Which came first? Tell me, you or me?

SENSELESS

I heard a brilliant sunset,
I saw a thunderclap,
I touched a piece of music,
Got a taste for travelling from a map.

I drank in a late night movie,
I listened to a book,
I watched a glass of red red wine
And grasped the call of a rook.

I sniffed a summer heat wave
And heard the cold in the fall,
Devoured the flowers that surged with spring,
Feasted my eyes on them all.

RIGHT AS RAIN

Right as rain
And sure as stone,
Smooth as sun
And warm as home.

Long as leaves
And salt as sea,
Broad as bird
And bright as bee.

Weird as weather,
Grand as gusts,
High as summer,
Low as dusk.

New as autumn,
Lost as hope,
Young as year
And old as rope.

ODE TO BLUE TACK

Oh think of the myriad things you can do
When you are sticky and stringy and blue,
Just think of it, how would it be if we lacked
The adhesive known as Blue Tack?

Men relish the odd jobs that you can perform
On non-porous surfaces when you're on form,
Like sticking up posters or photos or maps,
Or sticking down ashtrays or keys, perhaps.

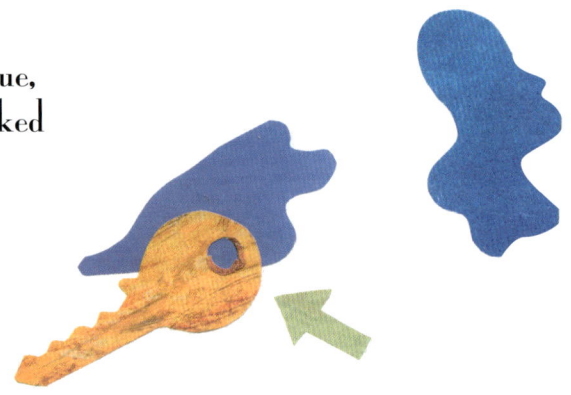

And though many don't know it you also clean fluff
From fabric and crevices, which can be quite tough.

Oh Blue Tack, oh Blue Tack, oh bluey blue blue,
You're sure as the seasons and cows that go moo,
Oh Blue Tack, oh Blue Tack, oh tacky tack tack,
I realise I've run out and I want you back.

You could have been green, you could have been red,
You could have been just a thought in someone's head,
You're humble, you're shapeless, you probably taste bad
But you are the best friend a note ever had.

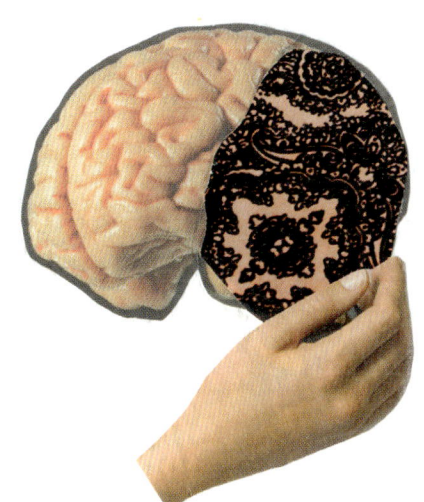

PIECE OF MIND

Give me a piece of your mind
Till I place it on my brain;
If it doesn't implore my IQ to soar
At least it will keep off the rain.

Pass me a part of your heart
And I'll put it in my chest;
If I start to hum it should start to drum;
Let's put it to the test.

If you gave me a taste of your tongue
It would scold my world with scorn;
I'd regret that I ever had any endeavour,
Regret that I ever was born.

RHYME IS THE REASON

Rhyme is the reason that hot air balloons
Dishevel the sky just like "not there" cartoons.

Rhyme is the reason that puppy-dog tails
Taste good in a potion with earthworms and snails.

Poems are the purpose that winds up the world
And watches it spin around, watches it twirl.

Poems are the purpose behind nightingales,
Big oak trees and honey bees and cute killer whales!

Rhyme is the reason that October winds
Arrive in midsummer to knock over things.

Rhyme is the reason that oceans of wine
Float pineapples, passion fruit, lemons and limes.

Poems are the purpose behind every tear,
Every dream, every doubt, every hope, every fear.

Poems are the purpose that prop up the sky;
May God strike me dead if I do tell a lie!

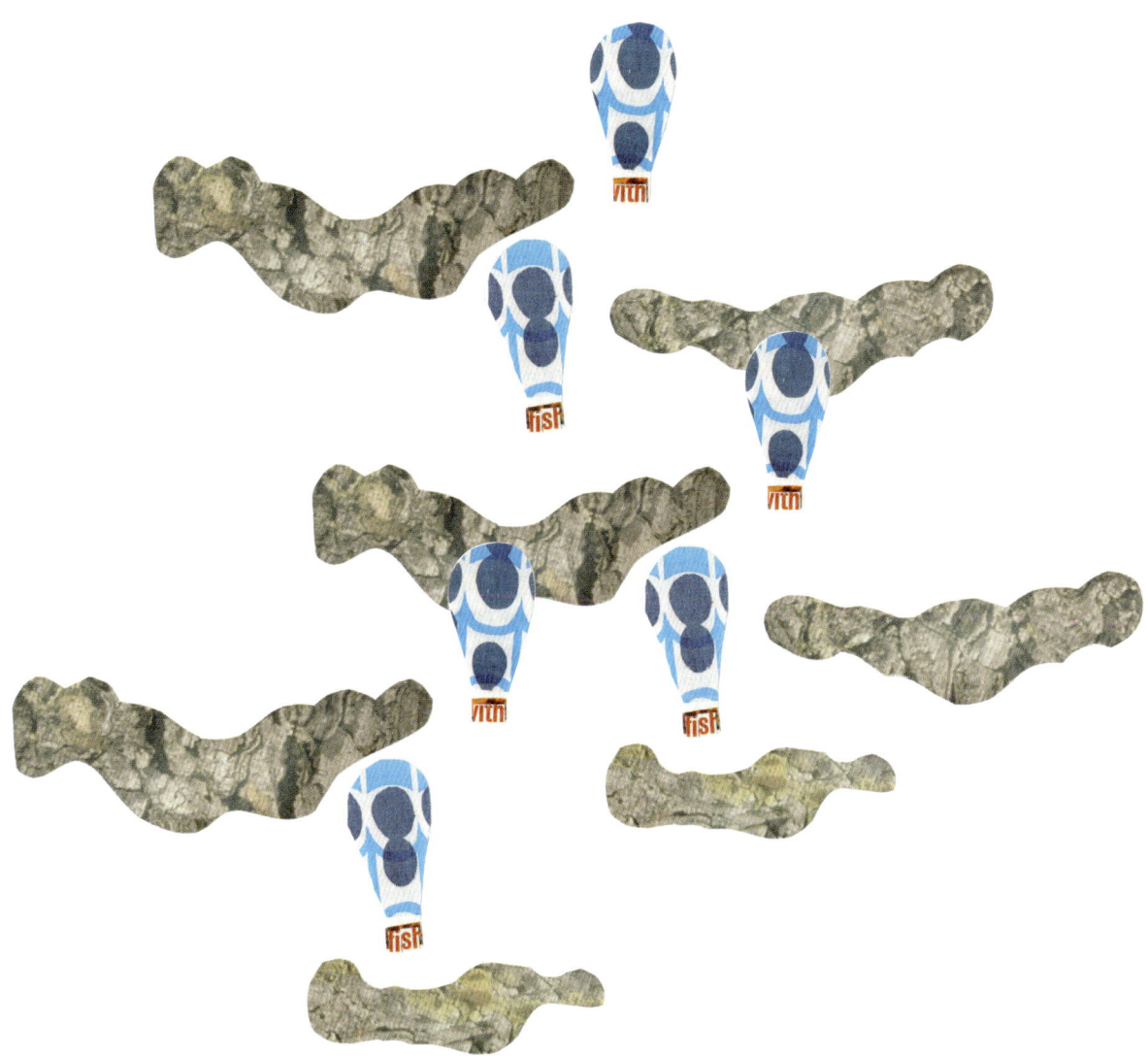

GREEN VEGETABLES

Green vegetables start to fly.
Green vegetables floating by.
Green vegetables from my plate.
Green vegetables it's too late.
They're gone!

Green vegetables in the sky.
Green vegetables don't know why.
Unidentified flying peas,
Courgettes and broccoli, what a wheeze!

Green vegetables on a date.
Green vegetables it's past eight.
Green vegetables please come back
Green vegetables to our shack.

Green vegetables drifting high.
Green vegetables rub my eyes.
Time to fetch a net methinks
Before they slip beyond the brink.
Too late!

Green vegetables lost in space.
Green vegetables interlaced
With galaxies and nebulae;
Food looks fruity in this sky.
Come down!

Green vegetables sober up.
Green vegetables time to drop.
Time to come back down to earth
So we can get our money's worth.

Green vegetables one more time
Green vegetables in this rhyme.
Floating's funny for a while
But levitation's not your style.

So please come back,
Cut out that crack,
Jump in your sack
And let us roast you
ON A RACK.

HELL IS HOMEWORK

Hell is Homework and Homework is Hell;
I dash from our school at the sound of the bell,
But what greets my feet when they make it back home?
A cruel clutch of hours with a mountain of tomes.

Hell is Homework and Homework is Hell,
I scream it, I shout it, I whinge and I yell!
A blizzard of bad set by Satan himself,
Skulking in our teachers mind like an elf.

Maths is a miserable mystery;
It's gruelling, it's galling, I'm doodling and dawdling.
Geography jumps all over me;
It's a pain in the neck, like being stretched on a rack!

Weekends are wonderous when they arrive,
No need to suffocate, no need to strive,
Just sit back calmly from nine until five,
After you've buried your schoolbag-alive!

I'd burn all the books but I'd just get bad looks
And a fresh batch of blight for my sins,
You can't win!

So listen old Nick, a quick word in your ear,
If you're big on cruelty and torture and fear,
Don't bother with hellfire, tridents and whips,
Instead why not try these few quick handy tips?

Set the damned essays and sums and the like,
Make them intolerably hard for the tykes,
Soon they'll change seamlessly from sinning cheats
To snivelling wee school kids with you as their teach!

FUNNY PHRASES

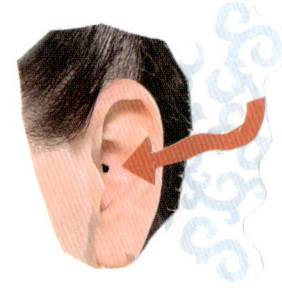

"He's a flea in his ear",
But who put it there?
The people who think up our language I hear;
They thought of a phrase,
It was really a craze,
And wrote it down in a big book one fine year;
The ear existed in ancient times,
The flea was a feature of archaic rhymes,
But never before were the two brought together,
Yet now they are partners for ever and ever,
Till death does its dance, they'll go per chance…

"You've a bee in your bonnet",
Lets not dwell upon it
Except to say that it was one time decreed
That bee should meet bonnet 'cos that's what they need,
To join in sweet marriage and make a big fuss
'Cos things just ain't just;
The bee was a-buzzing for many a mile,
The bonnet paraded itself with great style
And during an afternoon they did collide,
It can't be denied…

"I've a bug in my boot",
But what is the root?
'Cos I went in the garden to fetch me some fruit?
Or is it because it's a fancy expression?
That's not my impression,
In fact dear old reader we have a confession,
The above don't exist as a phrase as of yet,
It hasn't been let…

The fleas, bees and bugs have all gathered together
To decide the fate of our tongue,
They're sure to disqualify any odd phrase
That they think's been uttered all wrong.
A bonnet, an ear and the odd boot or two
Have turned up there too we can tell,
Let's hope they all sort out this dizzy debacle,
That everything wrong turns out well!

OUR DOG IS DREAMING

Our dog is dreaming that he is awake;
He drinks from a bowl that turns into a lake,
He's found a whole mountain of bones, stored away,
Its peak is a mile high, its his lucky day.

Our dog is dreaming that he is a cat,
An owl, a shrewd nighthawk, a vampire bat.
He's lost all his dogness in nocturnal games,
He's found a new neighbourhood, found a new name.

Our dog is sniffing the night in his dreams,
Wandering wonderstruck into its scheme;
He's chatting with jackals, whistling at a fox,
He's sleeping and creeping inside of his box.

Our dog is dreaming now all of the time,
He's lost all his day hours, he's left them behind;
He's entered a carnival off a weird track,
One day he'll end up there and he won't come back.

YOUR COMMON-OR-GARDEN MARTIAN

Your Common-or-Garden Martian has three eyes in his head,
Seven ears and twenty limbs a-dangling from his bed,
He holidays near Jupiter and breakfasts on the moon
And he visits his scaly mother-in-law in the month of June.

Your Common-or-Garden Martian thinks that life is a beach
With silver sand and polka-dot shells and waves that really greet a fella,
He sails the stellar on a sea of galaxies and such,
And smokes without a cigarette (but doesn't drink too much).

He's perfectly at home, in London or in Rome,
But he really likes to swim the stars, so he's not on the phone…

Your Common-or-Garden Martian is a happy-go-lucky chap,
With kids, a wife, a house, a bug-eyed monster in his lap,
He has a steady job that wobbles once in a wee while,
And by the way he gibbers you can tell he has real style.

All Common-or-Garden Martians think that flowers are junk food,
And that gravel is jewellery and valuable to boot,
They're frightened by our circus clowns and laugh at horror films,
And don't go giving them medicine as it only makes them ill.

They're perfectly at ease, in Paris or Berlin,
So long as they've got a shiny pot, a ship to go there in…

Your Common-or-Garden Martian hangs with earthlings now and then,
He's not in with the in-crowd but he has a pal called Ken,
He's weird as worms, it's true, in fact there really is no doubt
That Your Common or Garden Martian is pretty spaced out!

BUTTONS AND PUDDLES AND MUD AND CHAIRS

Buttons and Puddles and Mud and Chairs,
Telescopes, tweezers and gruel,
All co-exist in an off-the-wall world
Peopled by princes and fools.

Bedspreads and barnacles, toasters and terns,
Anchovies, art books and more
Muck in together in all kinds of weather,
So goes the relevant lore.

Wombats and warlords and witches and warts,
Demigods, dullards and doom
Are waiting to take control of this wide world
Waiting in some darkened room.

But birthday cards, bath bubbles, toadstools and tyres,
Cream cheese and cake knives and co.
Are saving the day in a roundabout way,
And that's about all that I know.

THE PINEAPPLE REPUBLIC

Out the back garden where all is green
We're creating a country that can't be seen;
A Pineapple Republic it is
With cakes and drinks with lots of fizz.

Out in the dirt by the washing line
We're building an island whose rules are fine;
They're unsullied by the muck of the know,
We're out here now and we're on our own!

Jack is parading a flag on a stick;
His face is proud and his steps are quick.
Laura is queen of the honey bees;
If you want asylum, down on your knees!

Out in the out-back we're running wild,
We've overthrown grown-ups, the state is a child;
We've declared independence but nobody knows;
One man one gobstopper, that's how it goes!

Here in the grandeur of giddy dreams
Birds alight on our grassy schemes,
Worms are watching us make laws up
And the whole world shines like a big gold cup.

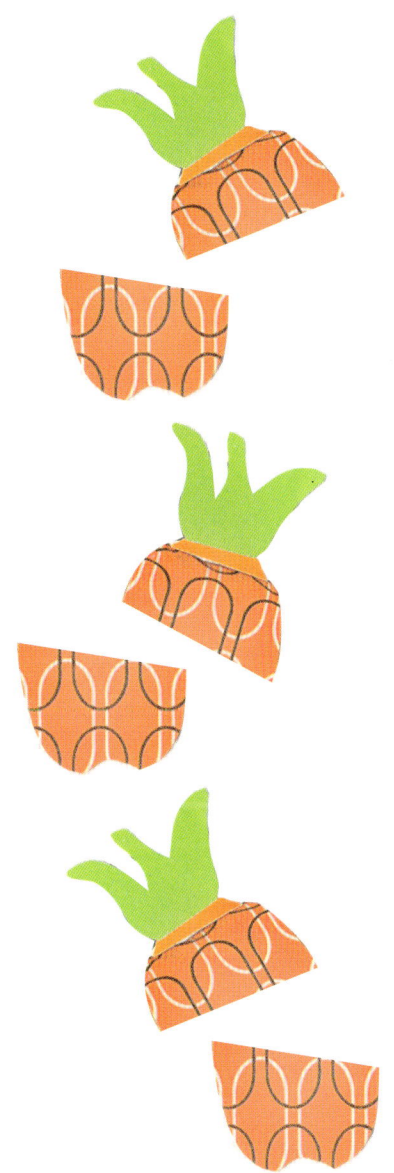

 THE END

Previously Published by Alan Murphy
The Mona Lisa's On Our Fridge

The Mona Lisa's on our Fridge is an off-the-wall collection of poems for youngsters populated by hippies, aliens, painters and octopuses! If you've ever wondered what flowers are about, how good sea creatures are at maths or what really happens to our rubbish when we put it out, this is the book for you. Full of the author's own trademark illustrations, this magical, surreal and outrageously funny book takes the reader into uncharted waters and provides a new perspective on the child's world. And like many a canny nursery rhyme its different layers of meaning give it plenty of cross-over appeal for adults.

To view extracts visit
www.avantcardpublications.com

PRAISE FOR "THE MONA LISA'S ON OUR FRIDGE"

"A celebration of imagination and wit"
Robert Dunbar, children's books of the year (2009)

"Many of the poems' titles reflect the wild exploration of fantasy within…they tiptoe adroitly into the child's world to comment from the inside…[they] won't change our messy world but they provide a better picture of it."
Dungarvan Observer

"An Irish poet makes his debut with this eye-catching and ear-bending collection-and provides the colourfully and appropriately surreal collage illustrations as well. Encompassing such subjects as The Alien Binmen, The Devil's Hot Water Bottle, and Funk and Jazz, Murphy's poems are diverting journeys into the sort imaginative realm we might associate with a Picasso or a Chagall, both of whom are refrenced here: "So doff your hat but hold onto your head;/Just lose your logical limits instead". The wonderfully liberating consequenses of an abandonment of these "logical limits" are wittily delineated in Murphy's poems."

Robert Dunbar in the Irish Times, books of the year

"What a breath of fresh air! And with a bite to it's verse and illustration...Alan Murphy, writer and illustrator, takes a Monty Python route in verse for young readers. No straight edges and the words, as one poem is titled, all 'funk and jazz'."

Children's Books Ireland Bookfest 2009

"I love books like [this] that defy categorization. Is this a poetry book with collage illustrations, or is the whole thing a piece of art that just happens to look like a book? It doesn't really matter either way. There is a crazy wackiness about this publication that I really like. Full of non-sequitur and bizarre juxtapositions, there is a distinct surrealistic quality in both the art and the verse. Collages are all patterns and images or part images, cut from magazines to create new images that are as bizarre as the poems they accompany...All I can say is read it...relax the mind and enjoy!

Teresa Doran, Books Ireland

In The Pipeline!
Prometheus Unplugged

A rock-themed collection of poems and songs to knock your shoes and socks off. Tremble in awe at the sound of The Grateful Din, try to spot a Flea At A Rock Concert, get woken up by the Lullaby Rap. These entertainments and many more are on the bill. Roll up, by your ticket and enjoy the show.